Women of God, Women of the People

Women of God, Women of the People

Ada María Isasi-Díaz

Chalice Press
St. Louis, Missouri

Biblical quotations, unless otherwise noted, are from the *New Revised Standard Version Bible*, copyright 1989, Division of Christian Education of the National Council of the Churches of Christ in the USA. Used by permission.

Cover art: Judith Jones
Design: Lynne Condellone

10 9 8 7 6 5 4 3 2 1

Library of Congress Cataloging–in–Publication Data

Isasi-Díaz, Ada Maria.
    Women of God, women of the people : four Biblical meditations / by Ada María Isasi-Díaz.
        p.   cm.
    Includes bibliographical references.
    ISBN 0-8272-4233-6
    1. Women in the Bible.   2. Hispanic American women—Religious life.   3. Liberation theology.   I. Title
BS575.I82 1994   94-39928
220.9'2'082—dc20   CIP

Printed in the United States of America

Contents

*P*rologue

This book presents in written form the Bible studies delivered orally at the Tenth International Christian Women's Fellowship Quadrennial Assembly held at Purdue University on June 22-26, 1994. This written version came about for three reasons. First, the time allotted for the Bible studies was short and not all the material prepared for that occasion was presented. Second, the presentations were enthusiastically received by the participants and many of them asked for copies of what was presented. Third, a number of the women ministers at the Quadrennial Assembly indicated that a written version of the Bible studies would be very helpful for sermon preparation.

The idea of publishing the Bible studies came from David P. Polk, Chalice Press editor, who was present at the Quadrennial Assembly and saw the enthusiastic reception of the audience. I am grateful to David for seizing the moment and encouraging me to publish the Bible studies.

I want to thank Carol Q. Cosby for inviting me to be part of the Tenth ICWF Quadrennial Assembly. Thanks also to Susan Shank-Mix who suggested my name. I wish to thank Bonnie Frazier and Maureen Osuga, ICWF President and Vice President for the last four years. Their warm and firm style of leadership is indeed a call to all women to develop our own administrative and empowering gifts as ministers, whether we are ordained or not.

Thank you to the Reverend Clarice Friedline who preceded me at each of the Bible study sessions. Her dramatic presentations of each of the women in the four biblical texts used were insightful and powerful and provided me with a most creative backdrop against which to do my own presentations.

Finally, I want to thank the many Quadrennial participants who were kind enough to come up to me during the assembly to let me know they appreciated the Bible studies. Being at the Quadrennial Assembly was a very affirming experience for me and it makes me rejoice once again in the power and commitment of women who take seriously the Gospel message of justice and peace. They are indeed *Women of God—Women of the People.*

Introduction

Before writing up the biblical meditations delivered at the Tenth ICWF Quadrennial Assembly, I need to explain the differences I find between an oral presentation and a written text, and the perspective from which I approach the Bible.

Orality and the Written Text

This material was developed to be presented at an assembly of almost four thousand women. To commit this material to a written form is both an act of faith and an act of hope on my part. I believe that though this written version will not have the same impact as its oral presentation, still it will be a useful resource for personal as well as group reflection. I hope that knowing this is a transcription of oral presentations will help the reader to fill in the gaps I purposefully crafted in these Bible studies as devices needed when people hear instead of reading something. Three things are important to understand in this regard.

First, I developed these Bible studies knowing that they did not need to stand alone. Not only did I know that Clarice Friedline would provide powerful dramatizations of the four biblical women before each of my talks, but I also knew that I could count on dynamic and insightful presentations by the keynote speakers. I also knew that I would be presenting these studies within a liturgical framework, for each plenary gathering at the assembly was designed to be a ritual having as its goal the enabling of understanding, commitment, and celebration.

Second, though in many ways when one writes for publication one has to take into consideration the reader, an oral presentation cannot be conceptualized apart from the listener. When I "write" an oral presentation, I am aware that I will sense whether the audience is understanding, is following what I am saying. I know I will have the opportunity to explain further, to give another example if need be. Furthermore, oral presentations are crafted in a somewhat colloquial language, and *what* is said is not distinguishable from *how* it is said. In other words, meaning is conveyed not only by the words but also by the tone of voice and the body language of the speaker as well as the mood of the audience as a whole.

Third, when one writes something one knows that it will take on a life of its own. Oral presentations, on the other hand, are crafted keeping in mind that they are attached to the speaker and the moment of delivery. These Bible studies were designed to be interpreted by me as the speaker for Disciples of Christ women who are concerned with living their faith. Turning them into written text freezes the words, the thoughts, the insights and separates the text not only from the author but also from the audience for which it was intended. Oral presentations and written texts are indeed two different forms of communication and are, therefore, created differently.

So turning oral presentations into written texts is always a risky business. What was intended to be heard is now to be read, what was conceived as part of a much larger whole is presented here in isolated fashion. In this written version only *what* is said will count, even if *how* it was said was part of what was meant. And yet I believe the written form of these Bible studies are a good resource for the readers.[1]

Using the Scriptures from a MUJERISTA Perspective[2]

In order for the reader to understand better the Bible meditations presented here, it is important for me to explain how I approach the Bible—what is my perspective, the lens through which I read the Bible. Key to my perspective is the fact that I am a *mujerista*—a Latina woman who struggles for my liberation and the liberation of all Latina women.[3] It is precisely this struggle for liberation, Latina women's struggle for survival, that constitutes the lens through which I read and interpret the Bible. To understand my and other *mujeristas'* interpretation of the Bible, one needs to know that we believe our *proyecto histórico* (historical project), our preferred future, is an intrinsic part of the unfolding of the kin-dom of God.[4]

The criterion that guides Latinas' usage of the Bible is *need*. We use the Bible when we need it, for what we need it, in the manner we need it. In reality though some today might denounce this, the fact is that all who approach the Bible do so from their own perspective, as a response to some need they have and that they think the Bible can help them with.

For Latinas, those in the Bible who struggled for liberation, for survival, including Jesus, are one of the few "reality checks" that Latinas have.

Society questions our reality, how we understand it and deal with it. Society alienates Latinas and marginalizes us because our cultural values and understandings are different. We are not willing to participate in society on the terms of the dominant culture because those terms are oppressive for us as well as for other marginalized groups. Anyone, including biblical persons, who has gone through situations similar to ours serves as an encouragement to us to believe in ourselves and our communities. All such persons and examples help us know that we are not imagining things; that though we are often rendered invisible by those who have power, we do not cease to exist.

The sense that the people of various Bible stories can understand us because they have also had to struggle for survival is important to Latinas. These stories become *ours* when we use them because we need them. To make them helpful in a given situation, we might change different elements of the story itself, or add elements from another pericope to the one being discussed.[5] For example, a Latina speaker at a national conference decided to use a Bible story to explain that we women needed to insist on our rights. To do so she mixed elements of the story of "The Woman with the Flow of Blood" (Luke 8:43–48) with the story of "The Uppity Woman" (Mark 7:24–30):

The woman in the Bible needed help. She realized Jesus could help her and nothing was going to stop her. It was not very nice, as a matter of fact, it was terrible of Jesus to tell her that she could not eat from the bread that was on the table. She could only have crumbs. If it had been me, I would have answered him that I have every right to eat from the bread on the table. We do not want just crumbs. No! (*applause*) Well, she insisted on her right, she took it without Jesus giving it to her. Jesus knew that power had gone out of him; and she had taken power in her own hands because she and her daughter were in great need.[6]

It is not that for Latinas the integrity of the biblical text is not important; it is that the need to survive, the need for liberation, takes precedence.

When we recognize how we are linked to people of the Bible we consider important, we extend our community to include those of ages past. We know our struggle for liberation is an ancient one; the Bible stories we use put us in touch with other ancient histories of struggle; they help us realize that as a community of struggle we have existed for many, many centuries. These biblical stories put us in contact with the communities of our forebears and teach us that though we must struggle with all our might against oppression, we must not grow weary.[7] By making us part of a much wider community of struggle biblical stories help us hold on to the belief that within the limited possibilities we have as marginalized people, *se hace lo que se puede*, one does what is possible. It helps us continue to understand that though we may not be able to solve problems or to remedy the terrible situation in which we live, we can make a positive contribution. Partial solutions are elements of the transformative change because the struggle to bring them about provides inspiration and can indeed provide the favorable conditions others need to be able to struggle for liberation.[8]

It is precisely this sense of the word of God that helps us struggle for survival, for liberation, that must be the critical lens through which *mujerista* theologians look at the Bible. How do we interpret and appropriate the Bible so that it becomes an effective tool in the struggle for liberation? We start by asserting that the interpretation, appropriation, and use of the Bible for Latina women has to enable and enhance our moral agency, our ability to be self-defining women. It cannot be pietistic and individualistic, concerned only with a private sense of salvation and used only for the consolation of the individual. This is why *mujeristas* reject fundamentalist interpretations of the Bible. Such usage has to be denounced whenever it oppresses Latinas or supports and promotes understandings and structures that oppress us.

As *mujeristas* we are concerned with the way the Bible is interpreted and used to reject or ignore an understanding of structural sin, the social implications of personal salvation, and the intrinsic relationship between struggle for survival, liberation, and salvation—between struggling for justice in this world and salvation and life everlasting. The Bible should help us to understand the oppression we suffer because of injustices in our world; the Bible should call us as a community of faith to struggle for justice so as to participate in the unfolding of the kin-dom of God.

For *mujerista* theology the enablement and enhancement of moral agency go hand-in-hand with a process of conscientization, an ongoing process of critical reflection on action that leads to a radical awareness of oppressive structures and their interconnectedness.[9] In this critical process the Bible should be used to learn how to learn—to involve the people in an "unending process of acquiring new pieces of information that multiply the previous store of information."[10] The Bible is a rich resource of "new information": stories of valiant women, of struggles against unbelievable odds, of communities of resistance, of women who found ways to survive in the midst of the worst oppression. This "new information" helps to reveal clearly problems that may have existed for a long time but ones we have failed to recognize. This usage of the Bible does not apply what the Bible says directly to our situations. But the Bible is seen as an important element in the formation of the moral character of Hispanic Women. The Bible can play an important role as Hispanic Women reflect on who we are as Christians and what are our attitudes, dispositions, goals, values, norms, and decisions.[11] But in the end it is the struggle to survive, the struggle for liberation, and not the Bible that is the source of moral values for Latinas, precisely because there cannot be—and even fundamentalists do not make—a direct application of the Bible to our everyday lives.

Conclusion

In the written presentation I have preserved off-the-cuff remarks, informal comments, colloquial expressions, and most of the opening remarks of each day when I tried to establish contact and continuity with the very large audience. I hope the reader who was not at the Quadrennial Assembly may sense the friendliness of the audience and my feeling that they were following me and ready always to hear more and be challenged further.

Notes

[1]For a very complete treatment of the differences between orality and literacy see two books by Walter J. Ong, SJ: *Orality and Literacy: The Technologizing of the Word* (London: Methuen, 1982); *The Presence of the Word* (New York: Simon & Schuster, 1970).

[2]For a much more complete explanation of a *mujerista's* perspective of Scriptures see Ada María Isasi-Díaz, "La Palabra de Dios en Nosotras—The Word of God in Us," in *Searching the Scriptures*, edited by Elisabeth Schussler-Fiorenza (New York: The Crossroad Publishing Company, 1993), 86-97.

[3]The concept of liberation has been much maligned. Liberation refers to the "for freedom Christ has set us free" of Galatians 5:1. Liberation is a process that has three different, interconnected aspects or levels: freedom from oppression at the social level, freedom from psychological oppression by struggling for self-fulfillment within the context of one's community, and freedom from sin. Liberation takes place within history; the history of salvation does not happen apart from day-to-day life. The unfolding of the kin-dom of God takes place in history through liberation. But liberation and the kin-dom of God are not one and the same thing. "Without the liberating events of history, the kingdom [*sic*] does not grow, but the process of liberation only destroys the roots of oppression and of the exploitation of one human being by another; this is not the same thing as the coming of the kingdom which is first and foremost a gift. It can even be said that historical, political, liberating actions mean the growth of the kingdom and are saving events; they are not, however, the coming of the kingdom, they do not represent complete salvation. They are historical embodiments of the kingdom and by that very fact also pointers toward the fullness of the kingdom; there precisely is the difference" (Gustavo Gutiérrez, *The Truth Shall Make You Free: Confrontations* [Maryknoll: Orbis Books, 1990], 16.) For a further explanation of the relationship between liberation and salvation see Gustavo Gutiérrez, *A Theology of Liberation: History, Politics, and Salvation.* (Maryknoll: Orbis Books, 1988), 83-105. See Ada María Isasi-Díaz and Yolanda Tarango, *Hispanic Women: Prophetic Voice in the Church* (Minneapolis: Fortress Press,

1992). See also Ada María Isasi-Díaz, *En La Lucha: Elaborating a Hispanic Women's Theology* (Minneapolis: Fortress Press, 1992).

⁴We use *kin-dom* instead of *kingdom* because the latter is obviously a sexist word that presumes that God is male; elitish—that is why we do not use *reign*. *Kin-dom* makes it clear that when the fullness of God becomes a reality, we will all be sisters and brothers—kin to each other.

⁵Though reader-response theories have helped us understand and explain how we relate to the text, they do not do so fully. In reader-response theories the text is central or, at least, the person is always seen in relation to the text. In our appropriation of biblical stories the text disappears as an element *per se* leaving only some of its elements present but always mediated through the need and usage of Hispanic Women. For an overview of reader-response theories see Jane P. Tompkins, ed., *Reader-Response Criticism,* Baltimore: The Johns Hopkins University Press, 1980.

⁶Quoted originally in Isasi-Díaz, "La Palabra de Dios," 88. Since whenever I give this kind of example, non-Hispanics seem to take it for granted that I am talking about a Latina with little formal education, let me say that the speaker to whom I refer here has a Ph.D. in literature. The mixing of elements from two different stories was not because she did not have knowledge of the Bible.

⁷My mother's understanding that the struggle is to live, *la vida es la lucha*, expresses this sense of ongoing resistance as a good and effective strategy in our struggle.

⁸For an excellent exposition on this subject see Sharon Welch, *A Feminist Ethic of Risk* (Minneapolis: Fortress Press, 1989), 74-81.

⁹For a fuller discussion of conscientization see Isasi-Díaz and Tarango, *Hispanic Women*, 94-110. For a different view that does not necessarily contradict this one see Justo Gonzales, *Manana: Christian Theology from a Hispanic Perspective* (Nashville: Abingdon Press, 1990), 75-87.

¹⁰Juan Luis Segundo, *The Liberation of Theology* (Maryknoll: Orbis Books, 1982), 121.

¹¹Charles Curran, *Catholic Moral Theology in Dialogue* (Notre Dame: Fides Publishers, Inc., 1972), 70.

*E*ve:
Mother of Humankind

Genesis 1:26—2:3

In the beginning, Eve: Eve our mother, our daughter, our niece, our sister, our friend, our committed partner, our grandmother. *Eva, la madre de la humanidad*, and, as a mother she does not only give birth but also nurtures, encourages, demands of us, today, this morning. Eve asks us:

- What did you hear last night that challenged you?[1]
- Or, did you neutralize everything and "feel good" instead of being challenged?
- What did you have to say yes to, what did you have to say a new yes to last night?

And today, I want you to promise yourselves that you are going to spend the day today looking for what you can say yes to. What is new to you? What challenges you? What can you say *sí* to?

Within this framework let us now turn to a study of scriptures, to a study of the texts in Genesis that refer to Eve.

When I took the introductory seminary course on the Bible I was surprised by the fact that only in the very last class of the semester did we turn to the story of creation. In reality, my professor, a well-known scholar, was simply making a very important point.[2] She wanted to point out that the stories of creation we find in the Bible were not written at the beginning of the history of the people of Israel. The accounts of creation found in Genesis in reality are a "looking back" to the origins of Israel by the Israelites themselves. These stories are an attempt by the Israelites to ground their lives and their reality in Yahweh, their God. These stories are not an objective view of what happened at the beginning. The stories of creation, in chapters 1 and 2 respectively, are different. Each one has its own particularities because they were written by different groups of people within the nation of Israel and for different purposes.

As we all well know, there is great variety in the Bible and whenever we confront its text we come away enlightened and puzzled, consoled and disturbed, embraced and challenged: the Bible is indeed a two-edged sword. One of the things that we often tend to ignore when we approach the Bible is ourselves—each individual reader. What are our questions? What is our world view? What are our values? What is our understanding of right and wrong?

So, during the days of this Quadrennial Assembly, I want to suggest that we use our time together to find out about how we approach the Bible. Through what lens do we read the Bible? We all come to the reading of the Bible with a history, with our idiosyncrasies, with our ideologies. The Bible does not speak in only one way. The Bible speaks to you, and to you, and to you, and to me. And the Bible does not speak the same to different ones of us.

Today a passage from the Bible might say something to you that it will not say tomorrow, not because the Bible changes but because you change, I change. We understand the Bible from the perspective of our contemporary world. At the same time, we view our world today often in light of our understanding of the Bible.

On this, the first full day of the assembly, we look at Eve, or rather, we look at how we look at Eve. When we read the stories of Eve, what do we want to know? Why do we read the story of cre-

ation, the story of Eve? What do we see? Who is
Eve for us? What does she say to us today?

In Genesis, chapter 1, verse 27, we read that Eve
was made in the image and likeness of God. The
decision to create Eve was not a light decision, a
spur-of-the-moment decision on God's part. In verse
26, the text reads, "And God said: 'Let us make
humankind in our image, after our likeness.'"[3]

Let us consider two points here. First, the "us"
in this verse is an indication of deliberation on
God's part. It is the only place in this account
where God speaks directly, and that points to the
importance of what is being said in this verse, of
the action that it announces. Second, we need to
look at the fact that the creature that God creates
after this deliberation, this creature is modeled
after God. Eve is created to be like God, to resemble God. This is something she shares with
Adam and with no other creature.

The phrase "image of God" is the guiding metaphor in this text. So we ask, what is created in
God's image? The answer yields the second element of the metaphor, bringing the metaphor to
life: male and female are created in the image and
likeness of God.

In this account there is no derivative sense con-
cerning the creation of woman. What makes us
think woman was an afterthought? This errone-
ous sense comes from rendering the Hebrew word

hā-'ādam, from translating this word by the English word *man.* But look carefully at Genesis 1:26 and you will see that translating *hā-'ādam* with the word *humankind* fits better. Why would God say "let us make man," and then make male and female beings? The text says, "let us make *hā-'ādam,*" humankind, and then makes clear that there are two kinds of humans: "male and female (*zākār ûn eqeba*) God created them."[4]

Why my insistence on all of this? Because we need to be very clear about the fact that in our woman-ness we image God. Because we are images of God not only in what we share with men: intellect, will, intelligence, soul. We also image God in our bodies. So if we as women are made in the image God, then God can indeed be imaged as woman as much as God is imaged as man.

Our images of God are based on us, on our world, on what we think. We are part of the metaphors through which we try to understand God. And, from the very beginning, in a very deliberate way, the stories of creation include woman-ness as a good metaphor for thinking about God precisely because we are created in God's image: our woman-ness is the image of God.

And what about the general understanding that Eve was a temptress? Was she a temptress? Did Eve introduce sin into human history? To answer this question we have to look at the second story of creation: Genesis 2:25—3:7. Here are a few pointers for an in-depth reading of this story of creation.

—Notice that Genesis 2:25 makes clear that the human body, our women bodies, are good: they are not a source of shame. The reference to nakedness as something Eve is not ashamed of indicates the goodness of our womenbodies and of all related to our bodies, including genital sexuality.

—Certainly the text, written by Israelites for the purpose, among others, of explaining the way they understood and valued or did not value women, shows Eve as being disobedient. But if you read the text suspending the judgment of disobedience, what you have here is an intelligent woman, a curious woman who investigates, who takes risks, who engages in discussion. Eve is a woman who wants to know.

—Observe that Eve does not discuss the matter of eating the fruit with her man. She does not ask his permission nor his advice. But neither is she secretive, deceptive. He is there and in his presence she thinks, argues with the serpent, decides, and acts.

—For sure, she is no temptress. The text simply indicates that she took, she ate, she gave it to him. The story does not say that he was reluctant, that he hesitated and she insisted. The text does not say she seduced him. She simply gave it to him. He is the one who is passive, who does not think: he takes the fruit and he eats it.

Today *we* look at Eve. *We* are women who like her are made in God's image and women who like her are thought to be secondary, derivative. Today *we* look at Eve as women who are considered less capable than men to lead in society, in our churches. We, women who struggle to bring about justice and peace for ourselves and our sisters, we must look at Eve. We look at her and try to discover in the biblical texts about her the hidden meanings, meanings obscured by the patriarchal world in which the text was written, the patriarchal worlds in which the text has been read throughout the ages, the patriarchal world in which we live today.

And Eve teaches us the goodness of our woman-ness, the goodness of our women bodies.

And because she was created in the image and likeness of God, because of that, we know that we can use ourselves, our woman-ness, as a metaphor for God. "Mother" is as good a metaphor for God as "father" is; and do not let anyone tell you differently. The woman searching for the lost coin in the Gospel is as good a metaphor for God as the shepherd looking for the lost sheep; and do not let anyone tell you differently. And a wise woman, Sophia, is as good a metaphor for God as a wise man with a white beard is; and do not let anyone tell you differently.

Why? Why are "mother," and the woman searching for the lost coin, and the wise woman, why are they good metaphors for God? Because Eve was created in God's image and like her, you and I, Eve's daughters, are created—body and soul—in the image of God.

Notes

[1] I am referring here to the challenging presentation of Dr. Emile Townes the first evening of the assembly.

[2] My professor was Phyllis Trible, Baldwin Professor of Sacred Literature, Union Theological Seminary, New York.

[3] This is the translation used by Dr. Trible. See Phyllis Trible, *God and the Rhetoric of Sexuality* (Philadelphia: Fortress Press, 1978), 13.

[4] Trible, 15-21.

A *Widow*
Who Believes in Herself

Luke 18:1–8

Continuing with the framework we explained yesterday, we want to set ourselves up to be challenged by the widow we read about in the eighteenth chapter of the Gospel of Luke. Being open to being challenged means that we make ourselves think, "Maybe what she is saying is right. Maybe I need to question what I think." That is all we need to be open-minded, and that is the mindset we want to have as we approach the widow Clarice Friedline so creatively and insightfully brought to life for us on this stage.

We need to understand the story found in Luke 18:1–8 against the background of Luke 11, where Jesus teaches his disciples to pray and follows it up with a declaration that if we ask, we will receive: if we who are not always so good find it impossible to say no to our children, much less will God say no to us if we ask. "Ask, and it will be given you; search, and you will find; knock, and the door will be opened for you" (11:9).

Ordinarily interpretations of this passage on the widow highlight exclusively the need we have to be insistent, to be importune, to be willing to bother others.

This is what we women have done throughout the ages, why we have been killed—because we are insistent, especially when the demand has to do with our children.

Today what we women need is to be sure of ourselves, to trust ourselves. Today when we insist on our rights, on our views, on our understandings of who God is and what God is like, we are usually met with derision. Our understanding of God, the ways we image God, come under scrutiny and are considered deficient, not good, even heretical, because they are ours, they are based on our woman-experience, on our woman-knowledge.

So, today, in these very difficult times for women in our churches, we look at the woman in this story, we look at the text and try to understand her, what she thought about herself, about her rights, about her own point of view. Today, given our situation, we want to look at this text and emphasize not only the widow's insistence but her character. What kind of woman was she? What kind of woman does it take to be insistent about justice for oneself, yes, justice for ourselves. This is about what the widow did to get justice for herself, to have her understanding prevail.

First, let us look at the position of the woman in this story.[1] Remember this is a parable, a fictional story Jesus weaves together to make a point. So every detail introduced in the story has a point. This woman is a widow. Widows in the Bible are objects of pity, recipients of favors. Living in a patriarchal society without a male to protect them and to be their point of reference, widows were victims of injustice. They were outsiders, no provisions were made by society for them, they were helpless and defenseless. Widows were overlooked in the Israelites' system of inheritance. They could remarry. The law of levirate marriage protected only widows who were daughters of priests by obliging the brothers of the defunct husband to marry the widow. But when there were no brothers, the widow was without recourse.[2]

The fact that the widow in this story approaches the judge herself indicates that most probably she had no male relatives since, if she did, they would have been the ones to advocate for her.

In our world today there are many women who resemble the situation in which the widow found herself. Today women continue to live longer than men so there are many more widows than widowers. Then there is the fact that today many more women choose to be single than women have in the past; today there is a significant increase of single mothers—all of these women who are not and choose not to be under the protection of men.

Like the widow in this parable these women have to speak for themselves, fight for themselves, face the patriarchal world in which we live by themselves, face our patriarchal churches by themselves—and all of this we do unprotected by any man. Yes, that is what we do, and we do it so often that we forget how much more work it is to be a woman in a patriarchal church, in a patriarchal society.

The second thing we notice in this story created by Jesus is that this woman, this widow, was a knowledgeable woman, a woman who knew that the law was on her side. Her appeal was legal. This is what the words of the judge mean: "Though I have no fear of God and no respect for anyone..." (Luke 18:46). He was ignoring either God's law or human law; or maybe he was ignoring both of them.

And looking at this text through today's assembly theme we have to say that we need to become knowledgeable about economics, we need to understand the economy of this country and how it intersects with and influences the economies of other countries. It is not beyond us, it is not something we cannot learn. Just as the widow could learn and understand the law so as to stand up against an unfair judge, so too can we learn about and understand economics in order to denounce injustice.

Third, this woman in Jesus' story is a most capable tactician. She carefully plots her strategy. She knows her adversary well: he does not respect the law, therefore, she does not try to reason with him but instead wears him down. No, women are not pests, women are not obnoxious. The problem is that faced with lack of integrity, faced with lack of respect for the law, faced with lack of willingness or ability to correct injustice, faced with such a situation, women have discovered that the best strategy is to pressure by being assertive, by being persistent, by repeatedly setting forth our demands.

Fourth, there had to be a moment when the widow said to herself: "I'm not going to accept the way things are. I'm not going to put up with it. I will risk being ridiculed, I will risk being called obnoxious. But I will do something about it." She knew that, given the situation she was in, to be right was not enough, to know the law was not enough. She realized that once she knew what was right she had to act on what she knew. This widow realized that to achieve what she wanted she had to *do*; she was concerned with justice through action.

Unfortunately many times we think that it is enough to know, that it is enough to pray, that it is enough to be concerned. But the widow shows us that we have to *do*. That is the true kernel of this story. And to *do* we have to know, we have to have courage, we have to decide, and then act. This widow acts out of moral strength and finds moral strength in acting.

Please, do not let anyone refer to this woman as the nagging widow. She is a woman of courage, a woman of action, and all of that because she knows.

My sisters, about ten years ago, I came to Purdue for a National Assembly of Church Women United and I heard a wonderful presentation that challenged me, challenged me, challenged me. Standing right here on this stage, on this side of the stage where I am, stood a woman of integrity, Marjorie Tuite. Margie, as we called her, talked to us about the burden of knowing. It is a burden to know because once you know you have to act. If not, you will betray yourself, your integrity will be eaten away, you will no longer be a moral person. The burden of knowing is a burden that calls for revolutionary integrity, it calls for consistent renewal of our commitment to follow the message of justice we find in the gospel. The revolutionary integrity to which knowing calls us is precisely that, a daily being converted to the core of the gospel message: to justice, to *doing* justice.

The widow Jesus tells us about in Luke 18 is a woman of revolutionary integrity. She knows what is right and aggressively goes out to get it.

The fifth point I want to make about this widow is the fact that she takes on someone in authority. You know how that is! You know how much we have been taught to follow those in authority, to go with what they say. One of my favorite bumperstickers is the one that says, "Question authority."

People in authority have to be held accountable; that is what the widow did. She said to the judge: "It is your job to see that justice is done, vindicate me against my adversaries."

How do we deal with people in authority? To hold them accountable is not a matter of ignoring them, disobeying them, or arguing with them. To hold those in authority accountable we have to be willing to engage them, to enter into dialogue with them. Any person in a position of authority who is not willing to dialogue should not have that position. But we also have to be open to the dialogue. Both, those in authority and those of us who do not hold such a position, have to listen intensively to each other. We have to listen until our ears ache and our heads are about to explode; we have to listen, attempting first of all to find a point of contact with the other.

The first step in this process of establishing dialogue with people in authority with whom we do not agree is to find in what the other person is saying something we understand, not agree with but understand. Can I at least understand why she thinks that way? The second step in this process is to find something we can agree with, even if it is not integral to what you are discussing but yet has some bearing on it. We all have done that. Many times in discussions or confrontations we have started by agreeing only on the fact that, "We need to have this resolved by five this afternoon." For example, in the negotiations to bring peace to El Salvador after ten years of civil war, the only initial point of agreement between the warring factions was that both sides recognized that neither side could win the war.

See, in the first step basic respect for each other is established. In the second step you begin to see the possibility of a fruitful dialogue because you taste a bit of the satisfaction of agreeing. Now, when dialogue is not embraced, it is either because one of the parties is like the judge in the parable—who seemingly knew the widow was right but either because he was lazy or because he had no respect for her, he did not want to rule in her favor—or dialogue is not embraced because one of the parties knows her arguments are weak, her reasons are not well-founded and this makes her afraid and insecure. Notice in the parable that the widow is willing to talk to the judge. The text says, "[She] kept coming to him and saying..." (18:3b). She kept the conversation going. In his case, however, apparently he just said no to her and then simply started talking to himself!

My sisters, the widow that Jesus carefully draws for us in this parable is indeed an audacious woman, a woman with the courage to *do* justice, not just to ask for justice to be done by others.

And here, to finish, I want to go back to the passage from Luke 11 to which I referred at the beginning. Notice that the passage starts with, "Ask and it will be given to you" (verse 9). But it does not stop there, it is not only a matter of asking. It is also a matter of doing: of seeking, of knocking. If we do that then we, like this widow, will be women of moral strength, of courage, of justice. We will not only ask for justice but we will be about *doing* justice. We will *do* justice because we have responsibly shouldered the burden of knowing, because we are women of revolutionary integrity, *mujeres de integridad revolucionaria*. Only then, only then, can we claim the widow of this parable as our sister.

Notes

[1]Rachel Conrad Wahlberg, *Jesus and the Freed Woman* (New York: Paulist Press, 1978), 104-127. Some of my insights in this biblical meditation are based on this powerful little book.

[2]O.J. Baab, "Inheritance," in *The Interpreter's Dictionary of the Bible*, Volume 2, edited by George Arthur Buttrick (Nashville: Abingdon Press, 1962), 701-703. See also the article by O.J. Baab on "Widows" in *The Interpreter's Dictionary of the Bible*, Volume 4, 842-843. Baab points out that the Hebrew word for "widow" resembles the word meaning "be mute," suggesting that widowhood induced a disgraceful muteness that might very well have been aggravated by the fact that widows wore identifying garments.

The *W*oman
with the Flow of Blood

Matthew 9:20–22;
Mark 5:25–34;
Luke 8:43–48

What do you have to report today? Were you challenged yesterday? What did you add to your burden of knowing? Remember the first night we were together here that Dr. Emile Townes told us that our diversity has outpaced our care for each other? Remember that she said we are losing our sense of "we"? Well, I think that our willingness to be challenged, our willingness to seriously consider what we hear even if we initially disagree, our willingness to say yes, well, I think this is a very important way to care for

41

each other, to learn to respect diversity, to learn to allow differences to touch us.

Now let us turn to one of my favorite Gospel passages: the woman with a flow of blood. And in this Bible study I will be using elements not only from Mark's version of this story but also Luke's and Matthew's versions.

Can you imagine what it would be like to have a vaginal hemorrhage for twelve years? Can you imagine what it would be like, on top of having a flow of blood for twelve years, on top of that, can you imagine what it is like to feel, to be considered to be, to believe that you are unclean? I want us to take a full minute in silence to imagine ourselves being considered by others and considering ourselves unclean.

This woman, everyone knew that this woman had a vaginal flow of blood.[1] Everyone knew it because according to the religious laws she was unclean and had to be ostracized. This woman was condemned by religious law to a feeling, a belief: she was condemned to believe that she was soiled and unworthy.[2] Not only was she unclean, but anything she touched was unclean. This meant it was her responsibility not to contaminate others. And we know that this was the way she felt because the text says that when she had to identify herself as the one who touched Jesus she "came in fear and trembling." She knew she was unclean and had hoped to pass *inapercibida*—she had hoped nobody would notice her. She knew that by touching the hem of Jesus' garment she had made him unclean. The story leaves no doubt about how she felt. She knew that now Jesus would have to observe some washing rituals in order to purify himself.[3] Can you imagine the state of mind of this person? She had indeed internalized the condemnation of her society and her religion. She had been socialized to think of herself as dirty, as soiled, as filthy.

I want us to think about this. Socialization is such a strong force in our lives. Even if we know differently "intellectually," we often act the way we have been socialized. Why? Because the process of socialization convinces us that what society says, what society has as a rule or custom, that is what is normal. If we think differently, if we act differently, we are deviants, we are abnormal. There is something wrong with us, we are inferior.

El proceso de socialización es tan fuerte, tan totalizante, que aunque intelectualmente sepamos que la verdad es otra, si actuamos en contra de lo que la sociedad considera normativo nos sentimos inseguras, nos sentimos mal. Lo que hacemos se considera divio, anormal, y a las que acutamos en forma diferente se nos considera inferiores.

It is against this socialization that this audacious woman has to act. What gave her the courage to act? What pushed her to go ahead and touch the hem of Jesus' garment despite her feelings of uncleanness? *Qué le dió a esta mujer audaz la fuerza para ir en contra del proceso de socialización?*

Matthew 5:26 tells us one reason, "she had endured much under physicians." Can you imagine twelve years of seeing doctors who did not know what to do? Can you imagine the kind of remedies they suggested? Is it far-fetched to think that she was financially ruined? Twelve years of seeing doctors would certainly push me to go against the grain, against any grain!

But I believe there was something else at work here. I think that what gave this woman the courage to come up behind Jesus and touch the hem of his garment was what is called the revolutionary potential of those who suffer, of those who are poor and oppressed, *el potencial revolucionario de los que sufren, de los pobres y los oprimidos.* It is not that she did not suffer; on the contrary, she did! But obviously this woman, at least at the moment when this story takes place, she did not understand herself primarily as suffering. She understood herself primarily as struggling against what oppressed her. What gave her confidence at this moment, what gave her strength, what gave her courage, was that she had not given up, that she still believed enough in herself to struggle. *La lucha, eso es lo que le da significado a la vida de esta mujer. Es el sentido de la lucha y no el hecho que sufre, es el luchar y no el sufrir, lo que la lleva a atreverse a tocar el manto de Jesús.*

Yes, it is *la lucha*, the struggle, that pushes her on, that gives her the strength to touch Jesus' garment. And because she is willing to struggle, because she calls forth from the depth of her being her own power, that is why she can benefit from Jesus' power.

In the version of this story in Luke's Gospel, you remember how Jesus responded. Everyone is pressing aginst Jesus. So to his question, "Who touched me?" Peter says, "Everyone is touching you, master." But that is not what Jesus was talking about. Someone had touched him in such a way that he perceived that power had gone out of him. This woman took the initiative. This woman dredged up from her battered self, from her sense of personal uncleanness, she dredged up a positive sense of self, of her life, of her body, of who she was. That positive sense of self, that was her power. And that power-touch of the woman was what Jesus felt. Her power called forth his; and he released his power.

My sisters, remember how the widow we looked at yesterday acted on her own behalf? Do you remember how we saw that she *did* for herself? We have the same thing here: a *doing* justice for oneself, something we women need to embrace.

Power, my sisters, is not given, power has to be taken.[4] *El poder es algo que tenemos que tomar, que tenemos que aceptar que tenemos; nadie nos puede dar poder.* Power is not bad. Power is neither moral nor immoral. It depends what we do with the power we have. We can use power to do good or to do evil. We can use power to create situations for people to be self-determining or we can use it to control and dominate others, to oppress others. *El poder en sí es algo neutral. Lo podemos usar para bien o para mal, para crear situaciones en las cuales las personas puedan ser sujetos de sus propias historias, o podemos usar el poder para controlar, para dominar y oprimir.*

The woman with the flow of blood used her power to access Jesus' power. And, as a result, she was healed. My sisters, we might try to give up our power, but we must not do that. To give up our power is to abdicate responsibility for who we are, what we do, who we become, and we, simply, cannot do that.

Let us go back and look at Eve. She had to decide for herself, she had to take responsibility for eating or not eating. God did not enclose the forbidden tree so as to curtail Eve's actions. At times we might think it would be better if decisions were made for us, if someone or something would tell us, "do this," "do not do that." But as part of our being made in the image and likeness of God we have to accept our power, we have to take responsibility for what we think, what we believe, what we decide.

Notice the interaction between Jesus and this woman. She uses her power, she takes the initiative. Jesus says, "Power has gone forth from me." This indicates that what happened to him in a way took him by surprise. And notice further that, according to Jesus, what healed her was her faith, the courage she mustered to touch the hem of his mantle, the power she had to access Jesus' power. *Es la fe de la mujer lo que la cura. Es el valor que tuvo de tocar el manto de Jesús; es el poder de la mujer lo que activa el poder de Jesús.* It is the asking accompanied by the doing, that's what is going on here.

All three accounts of this story use the phrase "made well" instead of "healed." This translates a Greek phrase that carries with it the idea of rescue from impending destruction by a superior power. And this is very important for us to notice because it gives us a window into perhaps one of the reasons this story was included in the Gospels. What is the impending destruction, the superior power this woman is fighting against? May I suggest that it is the casting off, the doing away with the ingrained blood taboo that classified her as unclean, that is what she is fighting against. The fact that all three Synoptic Gospels report this story signifies that in three different contexts of the early Christian community this event in the life of Jesus was considered important. Certainly Jesus rejects the uncleannness of women. The fact that all three evangelists interrupt the story of the raising of the daughter of Jairus—one of the leaders of the synagogue—indicates that the early community saw the event of the woman whose faith saved her from impending destruction as important.

This story, my sisters and brothers, is one of those gems that preserves for us a glimpse of what the early Christians meant by "[in Christ Jesus] there is no longer male and female" (Galatians 3:28). It meant that the Christians were a community of equals.[5] *Este evento en la vida de Jesús nos deja ver un poquito cómo era la comunidad primitiva de cristianos. Era una comunidad en la cual todos eran uno en Cristo Jesús; una comunidad en la cual las mujeres tanto como los hombres eran considerados capaces de tener las mismas capacidades y cualidades; una comunidad en la cual había igualdad.*

In this community of equals Junius, a woman, was as much an apostle as Paul; Phoebe and Prisca, both of them women, were deacons;[6] Mary Magdalen was the first witness of the resurrection of Jesus. This community of equals recognized that the women disciples of Jesus were the ones who paid for his personal needs and financially sustained his ministry;[7] and it was the women who stayed by the cross until the end.

What the women of the Gospels did then outlines for us what we are to do today. We must grab hold of our power and insist that our churches have to be communities of equals.

Al final, ya desesperada, lo último que le quedaba a esta mujer con el flujo de sangre era la lucha. Y convencida de que "sí se puede," luchó, usó su poder y se curó. Igual tenemos que hacer nosotras.

In the end, all this woman had left was her belief in the struggle. She realized that as long as she struggled there was hope, and that she had nothing to lose by trying.

May her faith in the struggle, her belief in herself regardless of all that society thought about her, be a source of inspiration, a source of blessing for us.

Notes

[1] You can read the laws that governed uncleanness for women in Chapters 12 and 15 of the book of Leviticus.

[2] The idea of uncleanness seems to have been a development of primitive taboos imposed on places, things, actions, and people that were considered potentially destructive to a group, a clan, a tribe. So laws of uncleanness are, first of all, related to a sense of self-preservation. Second, laws of uncleanness, especially those around issues of sexuality, life, and death arise from a sense that

potent and mysterious forces are at work and "anything repulsive, abnormal, or distorted was likely to be regarded as unclean." The third step seems to happen once the idea of deities has developed. Uncleanness is then related to the will of the gods: the unclean is repulsive to or prohibited by the gods (Isaiah 35:8; 52:1; Ezekiel 39:24; Revelation 21:27), or belongs to the sphere of the demonic powers opposed to the gods (Zechariah 13:2; Mark 1:23; Luke 4:33; Acts 5:16). Fourth, the laws governing cleanness and uncleanness are developed and rituals of purification are set and prescribed. In priestly thought uncleanness was considered to be contagious, so one could become unclean by contact with an unclean person or thing.

"A woman's menstrual flow, because of its cyclic occurrence analogous to such important cosmic rhythms as the phases of the moon, its connection with fertility, and its relationship to the life forces contained in the blood, was a potent source of uncleanness....Analogous to, but more serious than, menstrual impurity was a persistent discharge of blood from a woman." (L.E. Toombs, "Clean and Unclean," in *The Interpreter's Dictionary of the Bible,* Volume 1, edited by George Arthur Buttrick [Nashville: Abingdon Press, 1962], 641-648.)

[3]*Ibid.*, see particularly the section of this article dealing with "Purification Rituals."

[4]Several women came to me afterwards and asked me to amplify what I meant by this. Power has to do with self-actualization, with coming into one's own source of strength and being. Therefore, I believe that others can help us, enable us by affirming us and providing for us the opportunities we need to come to know ourselves, appreciate ourselves, value ourselves. But in the end, only each one of us can actualize ourselves, can value ourselves, can use our potential to its maximum in order to become as fully as possible the persons God intends us to be. Power has to do with ability to act and to influence others. And that is something that cannot be given to anyone.

[5]For ample explanation of this theme see Elisabeth Schussler-Fiorenza, *In Memory of Her* (New York: Crossroad 1983).

[6]Schussler-Fiorenza, chapter 5.

[7]Luke 8:1–3.

*M*ary—Woman of God, Woman of the People

Luke 1:46–55

My sisters, here we are, this glorious last morning of our time together. Is it not wonderful! I think times like these are "eschatological glimpses," glimpses of what the kin-dom of God will be like. *Eschatological* refers to the fullness of time when things, animals, the earth, humans, we all will have the opportunity to reach beyond, to become what, who, God intended us to be. So eschatological glimpses are moments in our lives when we have a sense of "this is what it is going to be like."

This assembly is an eschatological glimpse because we have reached beyond, we have listened, we have dialogued, we have shouldered the burden of knowing. This assembly is an eschatological glimpse because we leave empowered and ready to be evermore women of revolutionary integrity, women who *do* justice, women who stand in solidarity with the poor and the oppressed. Yes, this is what the kin-dom of God is like, *la familia de Dios. No uso la frase "reino de Dios" porque para mi Dios es amiga, es madre tanto como padre. Y "reino" es una palabra clasista.*

I use *kin-dom* instead of *kingdom* because *kingdom* is a sexist word referring to males, and it is a classist term that refers to monarchs. We are the family of God, the sisters and brothers of Jesus who *do* the will of God. We are God's kin because, as Patricia Tucker told us night before last, for us to be blessed means to be willing to risk, to be willing to risk in order to bring about justice.

Today our Bible study has to do with Mary. Mary, the mother of Jesus; Miriam of Nazareth; Mary, the bride of Joseph, and she married him![1] What a woman! As she said to us in the dramatization we just experienced, she was an insider, she was a disciple, the disciple *par excellence.*[2] I'm not sure the disciples of Jesus would have stuck together and made a go of it, followed The Way—as Christianity seems to have been known in the beginning—I think they might not have stayed together at the beginning had Mary not been there.

My favorite image of Mary is at the beginning of the book of Acts. The disciples are together at the upper room. The men in the group had run away when the going got difficult. They had failed Jesus; one of them had betrayed him and their leader had denied him. And now Jesus was not with them anymore, "When is he going to come back?" They keep wondering. So Mary gathers them, "Let's stay together," she says to them; "let's encourage each other, let's figure out together what we should do." And then, Pentecost takes place.

Mary of Nazareth, Mary the mother of Jesus, and for the early community—at least the community that is the context for the Gospel of Luke— Mary, the representative of the followers of Jesus. When in the Magnificat we hear her say, "All generations will call me blessed," this is not a boastful proclamation. For the Jewish people, in poems like this one, in proclamations, during their celebrations, the person speaking identified with the group, speaks for the group. In this poem, based on the song of Hannah in chapter 3 of 1 Samuel, what is to be called blessed is the group of Jesus' followers of which Mary is the prototypical disciple. This is the Mary, the follower of Jesus, who says the Magnificat. She is saying, "God has looked upon us with favor and we are blessed and will be blessed. We are God's people and Jesus has shown us what this God is like. And we have to be likewise." *María, la disícpula de Jesús por excelencia.*

As a second point of our study I want to look at verses 52–53 of the first chapter of Luke. What is this God to whom Jesus repeatedly pointed, what is this God like? What is this God whose family we are called to be, what is this God like? Well, this God puts down the mighty from their thrones and sends the rich away empty. This God, whose family we say we are, exalts the lowly and fills the hungry with good things. This God of Jesus and the God we Christians claim as our God makes a preferential option for the poor. And if we claim we are God's kin, then we have to do likewise. We have to opt for the poor, we have to cast our lot with the poor and the oppressed.[3] *El Dios de María, el Dios de Jesús, el Dios que los cristianos proclamos como nuestro Dios, hace una opción preferencial por los pobres.*

How do we opt for the poor? Let me suggest two ways that I believe we are to express our option for the poor. First, we have to denounce injustice. We have to call it as we see it through our Christian lens in our families, at our workplaces, in our churches, in our society, in our country. And what if our families dislike us, or worse yet, ignore us? What if we lose our jobs? What if our churches do not ordain us or revoke our orders? What if we are considered unpatriotic, anti-American? Like Eve we have to choose, and Mary's Magnificat makes clear that we have to opt for the poor, speak out against injustice, regardless of the consequences.

The second thing we need to do to opt for the poor the way the God of Mary, the God of Jesus does is this: we need to stop being so liberal and we need to become radical. We have to stop wanting to please others and be liked. We have to stop thinking that feeling guilty is enough. No, don't feel guilty; instead, do something to change the situation about which you are feeling guilty. For example, don't feel guilty about having certain privileges like education and money. Instead use your privileges to bring about justice for all. But, can I be honest with you? Bringing about justice necessarily means that we all are going to be affected. We are part of that tiny percentage of people in the world who eat three times a day, have roofs over our heads, get medical check-ups once a year. The resources in this world of ours are not infinite, and we must share if justice is to triumph. And remember, no justice, no kindom of God. So let us be radical, let's demand change, and let's start by demanding it of our own selves.

The third and last point I want to make this morning has to do with verses 48 and 50 in Luke 1.

This poem talks about generations: "from generation to generation."

Yesterday I talked about *la lucha*, the struggle. That is what gives meaning to the lives of the poor and the oppressed. And what the Magnificat always reminds me of is that God knows we need divine mercy, that we need it from generation to generation because the struggle is for the long haul, *que la lucha continúa de generación en generación.* It was precisely this understanding that led me to pay attention to the importance of the struggle. The struggle goes on; it has meaning in itself.

In many ways our job as women who struggle to do justice is to receive from the "mothers" of our different groups, different denominations— some of them sitting here in this hall with us today—to receive from them the struggle. We must be in touch with what they have done, with their vision. We do not start from scratch. We must not waste time by ignoring what they know, what they did, how they remember and understand what they did, how they see what we are doing and how they see the future.

After we receive the struggle from our "mothers" we must take that struggle and nourish it, put our own imprint on it. Our struggle for justice today, the struggle of this generation, includes issues and understandings that either were absent before or were present just in embryonic form. Issues having to do with ecology, with health, with economic justice: do not think the "mothers" did not struggle in these areas. But our task today is to add our own wisdom to theirs. Our task is to develop and implement strategies to bring about change according with the way institutions operate today, in ways that are effective, in ways that most probably will be different from the way things have been done before.

And in this process of struggling from generation to generation, our task is also to pass on the struggle to our daughters. Our task is to nurture the young ones, to welcome them and their viewpoints and ways of acting.

What understanding of the struggle do we pass on to our daughters, our nieces, our younger sisters, the new members of our churches, of our groups, of the staff? The text before us today tells us that the understanding we need to pass on is the one of option for the poor. It is the understanding that justice will flourish only if we opt for the poor and that our option for the poor impacts our lives, who we are, how we live, what we own, what our values and norms are.

The struggle today has taught us that it is impossible to separate charity, love, agape, from justice. And justice today means solidarity with the poor; it means that we embrace their struggle, their world-view; it means that we privilege their understandings about our world and about God.

My sisters, *la vida es la lucha, vivir es luchar y luchar es vivir*. To struggle is to live. For us Christians there is no living that is not a living to struggle for justice, a struggling to live justice.

My soul magnifies our God, a God for whom mercy and compassion are not possible without justice.

My soul magnifies our God and is ever grateful to the God of Mary, of Jesus, of our foremothers, of our sisters, of you, and you, and you, for having called me and for calling you to *la lucha*, to the struggle, to the struggle for justice.

Abracemos la lucha por la justicia. Entonces podremos ser la visión. Let us embrace the struggle for justice. Then we will be able to be the vision.

My sisters, *sí se puede*; it can be done, it must be done. To be Christians we must be women of justice. That is what being the vision is all about.

Notes

[1] An inspirational book for me on Mary is Ann Johnson, *Miryam of Nazareth* (Notre Dame: Ave Maria Press, 1984).

[2] Elisabeth Schussler Fiorenza, *In Memory of Her* (New York: Crossroad, 1983), 140-154.

[3]For further reading on the issue of option for the poor and solidarity with them, I recommend the following. Gustavo Gutiérrez, *The Power of the Poor in History* (Maryknoll: Orbis Books, 1983), Chapter 4, "The Historical Power of the Poor." Ada María Isasi-Díaz, "Solidarity: Love of Neighbor in the 1980s," in *Lift Every Voice*, eds. Susan Brooks Thistlethwaite and Mary Potter Engel, (San Francisco: Harper and Row, 1990), 31-40.